Changed to just a book   tape not replaced   2/4/2004   EAN.

Adventures in Storytelling

How Anansi Obtained the Sky God's Stories

An African Folktale from the Ashanti Tribe

Illustrated by
Janice Skivington

CHILDRENS PRESS ®
CHICAGO

Adventures in Storytelling

Dear Parents and Teachers,

Adventures in Storytelling Books have been designed to delight storytellers of all ages and to make world literature available to nonreaders as well as to those who speak English as a second language. The wordless format and accompanying audiocassette make it possible for both readers and nonreaders who are unacquainted with a specific ethnic folktale to use either the visual or the audio portion as an aid in understanding the story.

For additional reference the complete story text is printed in the back of the book, and post-story activities are suggested for those who enjoy more participation.

The history of storytelling

"Once upon a time . . . ."

"Long ago but not so long ago that we cannot remember . . . ."

"In the grey, grey beginnings of the world . . . ."

"And it came to pass, more years ago than I can tell you . . . ."

These are magic words. They open kingdoms and countries beyond our personal experiences and make the impossible possible and the miraculous, if not commonplace, at least not unexpected.

For hundreds of years people have been telling stories. You do it every day, every time you say, "You'll never believe what happened to me yesterday"; or "You know, something like that happened to my grandmother, but according to her, it went something like this . . . ."

Before video recorders, tape recorders, television, and radio, there was storytelling. It was the vehicle through which every culture remembered its past and kept alive its heritage. It was the way people explained life, shared events, and entertained themselves around the fire on dark, lonely nights. The stories they told evoked awe and respect for tradition, ritual, wisdom, and power; transmitted cultural taboos and teachings from generation to generation; and made people laugh at the foolishness in life or cry when confronted by life's tragedies.

As every culture had its stories, so too did each have its storytellers. In Africa they were called griots; in Ireland, seanachies; in France, troubadours; and in the majority of small towns and villages around the world they were simply known as the gifted. Often their stories were hundreds of years old. Some of them were told exactly as they had been told for centuries; others were changed often to reflect people's interests and where and how they lived.

With the coming of the printing press and the availability of printed texts, the traditional storyteller began to disappear — not altogether and not everywhere, however. There were pockets in the world where stories were kept alive by those who remembered them and believed in them. Although not traditional storytellers, these people continued to pass down folktales, even though the need for formal, professional storytelling was fading.

In the nineteenth century, the Grimm brothers made the folktale fashionable, and for the first time collections of tales from many countries became popular. Story collections by Andrew Lang, Joseph Jacobs, and Charles Perrault became the rage, with one important difference: these stories were written down to be read, not told aloud to be heard.

As the nineteenth century gave way to the twentieth, there was a revival of interest in storytelling. Spearheaded by children's librarians and schoolteachers, a new kind of storytelling evolved — one that was aimed specifically at children and connected to literature and reading. The form of literature most chosen by these librarians and teachers was the traditional folktale.

During this time prominent educator May Hill Arbuthnot wrote that children were a natural audience for folktales because the qualities found in these tales were those to which children normally responded in stories: brisk action, humor, and an appeal to a sense of justice. Later, folklorist Max Luthi supported this theory. He called the folktale a fundamental building block, an outstanding aid in child development, and the archetypal form of literature that lays the groundwork for all literature.

By the middle of the twentieth century, storytelling was seen as a way of exposing children to literature that they would not discover by themselves and of making written language accessible to those who could not read it by themselves. Storytelling became a method of promoting an understanding of other cultures and a means of strengthening the cultural awareness of the listening group; a way of creating that community of listeners that evolves when a diverse group listens to a tale well-told.

Many of these same reasons for storytelling are valid today — perhaps even more relevant than they were nearly one hundred years ago. Current research confirms what librarians and teachers have known all along — that storytelling provides a practical, effective, and enjoyable way to introduce children to literature while fostering a love of reading. It connects the child to the story and the book. Through storytelling, great literature (the classics, poetry, traditional folktales) comes alive; children learn to love language and experience the beauty of the spoken word, often before they master those words by reading them themselves.

Without exception, all cultures have accumulated a body of folktales that represent their history, beliefs, and language. Yet, while each culture's folktales are unique, they also are connected to the folktales of other cultures through the universality of themes contained within them. Some of the most common themes appearing in folktales around the world deal with good overcoming evil; the clever outwitting the strong; and happiness being the reward for kindness to strangers, the elderly, and the less fortunate. We hear these themes repeated in stories from quaint Irish villages along the Atlantic coast to tiny communities spread throughout the African veldt and from cities and towns of the industrialized Americas to the magnificent palaces of the emperors of China and Japan. It is these similarities that are fascinating; that help us to transcend the barriers of language, politics, custom, and religion; and that bind us together as "the folk" in folktales.

Using wordless picture books and audiocassettes

Every child is a natural storyteller. Children begin telling stories almost as soon as they learn to speak. The need to share what they experience and how they perceive life prompts them to organize their thoughts and express themselves in a way others will understand. But storytelling goes beyond the everyday need to communicate. Beyond the useful, storytelling can be developed into a skill that entertains and teaches. Using wordless picture books and audiocassettes aids in this process.

When children hear a story told, they are learning much about language, story structure, plot development, words, and the development of a "sense of story." Wordless books encourage readers to focus on pictures for the story line and the sequence of events, which builds children's visual skills. In time, the "visually literate" child will find it easier to develop verbal and written skills.

Because a wordless folktale book is not restricted by reading ability or educational level, it can be used as a tool in helping children and adults, both English and non-English speakers, as well as readers and nonreaders to understand or retell a story from their own rich, ethnic perspective. Listening to folktales told on an audiocassette or in person offers another advantage; it allows the listener, who may be restricted by reading limitations, to enjoy literature, learn about other cultures, and develop essential prereading skills. Furthermore, it gives them confidence to retell stories on their own and motivates them to learn to read them.

Something special happens when you tell a story; something special happens when you hear a story well-told. Storytelling is a unique, entertaining, and powerful art form, one that creates an intimate bond between storyteller and listener, past and present. To take a story and give it a new voice is an exhilarating experience; to watch someone else take that same story and make it his or her own is another.

Janice M. Del Negro
Children's Services
The Chicago Public Library

The following story is a favorite trickster tale from West Africa. Clever Anansi, who in this story appears as a spider, tries to retrieve all the stories of the world from Nyami, the powerful sky god. Anansi wins the stories, only to find that a trick has been played on him.

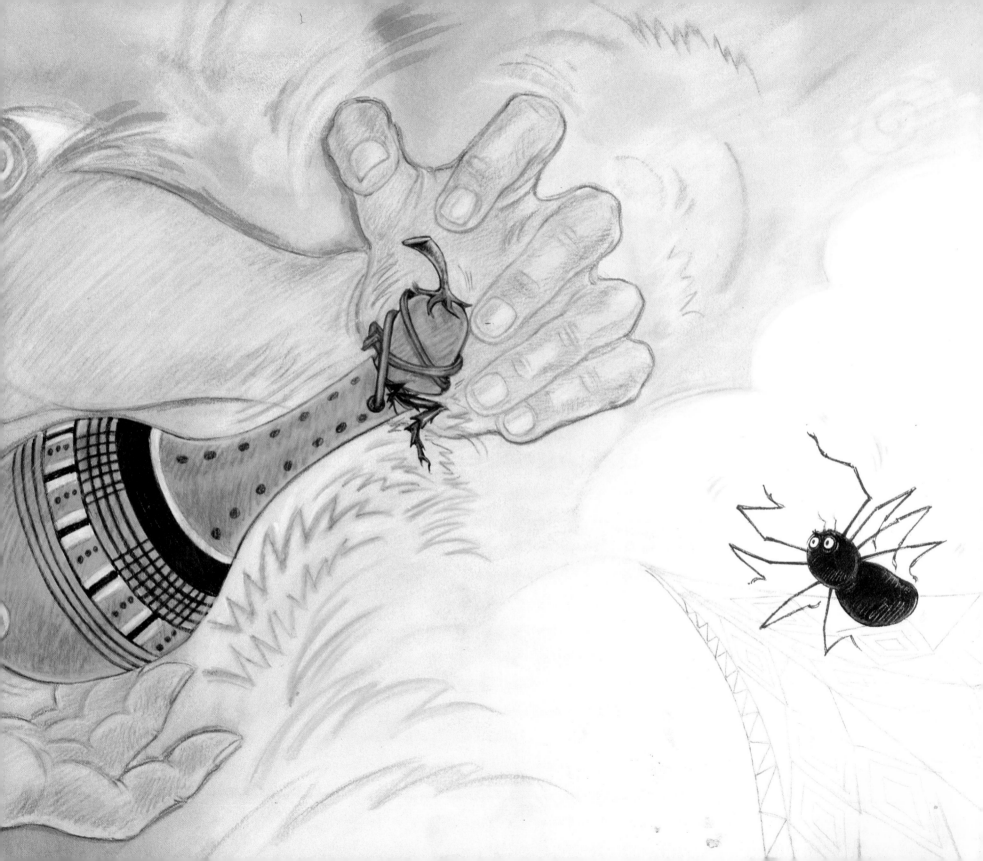

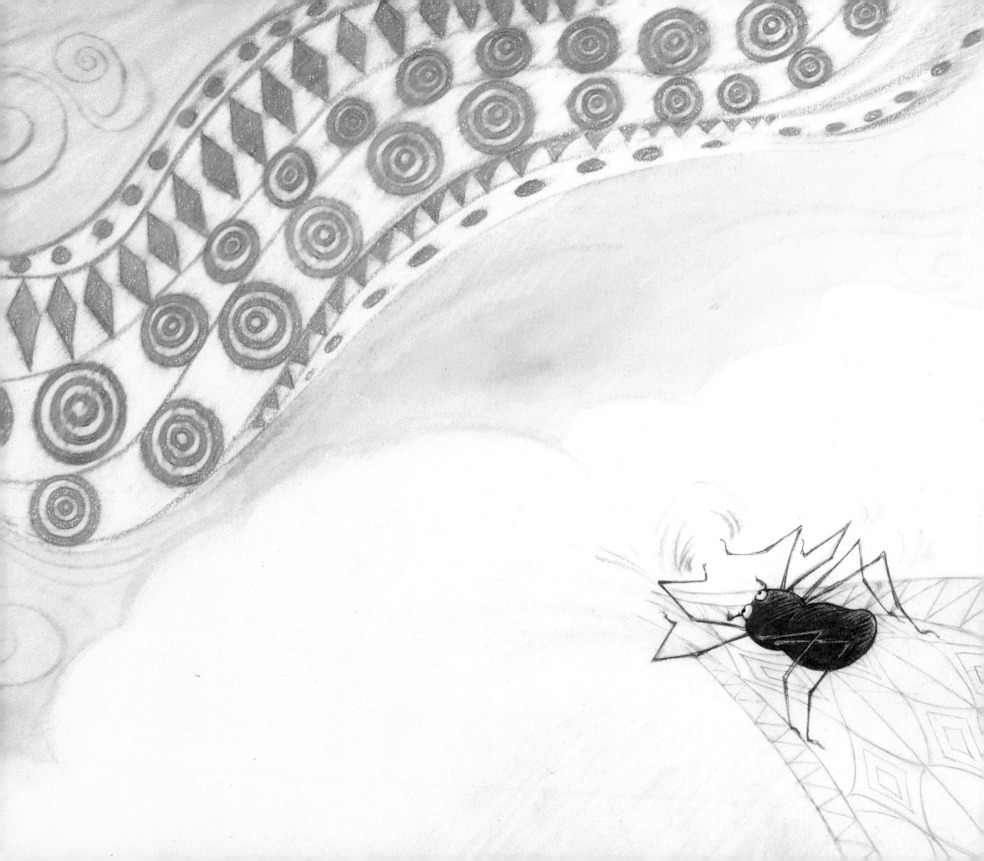

About the storyteller

My name is Donna Lanette Washington. I am the storyteller you hear on the tape recording of *How Anansi Obtained the Sky God's Stories*. I also am one of the characters in the story. The illustrator of this book has drawn me as a storyteller in a small African village.

I have loved stories ever since I was very young. Every night at dinnertime, during dessert, my father would sit at the head of the table and tell stories. That was when I discovered that I could travel around the world and through time without ever leaving my chair.

When I began college, the world of storytelling was reopened for me. Once again I could feel the magic of stories. It was at this time that I decided to bring the magic to others.

Since I graduated, I have shared many stories with many people. I hope you have enjoyed hearing the story about Anansi and will want to share it with others.

About the illustrator

My name is Janice Skivington. Creating the characters for this book has been a joy for me. You can see by the picture I have drawn of myself that each of the characters in the Anansi tale is especially close to me.

I developed my love for animals, even little spiders, while growing up in the Philippine Islands where my parents were missionaries. Even as a child, I liked to watch the lizards and insects around our house. After studying art in college, I began to illustrate children's books. Now I live in Wheaton, Illinois, with my husband and three children.

In addition to painting and drawing, reading books and traveling are interests of mine. Usually, before I begin to draw, I read about the people and places I'm going to illustrate. Afterward, I have the feeling that I've visited them without ever having left my studio.

Story text

Once all the stories in the world were collected in one place. Nyami the sky god held them all. Many people had come to try to buy the sky god's stories. But always, the price was too high— until Anansi the spider came to Nyami and asked to buy his stories.

"How can you, Anansi, hope to buy my stories," said Nyami.

"Braver creatures than you have tried and all of them have failed."

Anansi said to Nyami, "All I can do is try. Please tell me what I have to do?"

Nyami said, "Very well. You must bring me Momboro the hornet, Onini the python, and Osebo the leopard."

Anansi said, "Very well." And he went back down to earth. The first thing Anansi did was to get a large gourd and hollow it out. Then he filled it with water and took it over to where Momboro the hornet was flying around in the treetops.

Anansi sprinkled water all over Momboro and said, "Momboro, it's raining. Come into my gourd where you will be safe and dry."
Momboro said, "Thank you friend Anansi," and flew into the gourd.

Anansi then put on the top and carried it up to Nyami.

When Nyami saw Momboro he said, "My hands have touched it; but there remains what still remains."

And so Anansi went back down to earth. The next thing he did was to cut a long bamboo stick and lay it down beside the river. Before too long Onini the python came slithering by the bank. When Anansi saw him, Anansi began to have an argument with himself.

"He is longer. He is not longer. He is longer. He is not longer. He is longer. He is not longer."

Onini stopped slithering along and looked at Anansi.

"Friend Anansi, what are you doing?"

Anansi said, "Can't you see, I'm having an argument with my wife. She says that you're not as long as this bamboo pole, and I say you are. Would you do us a favor, Onini? Would you lay down beside this bamboo pole so we can measure which of you is longer?"

Onini was very flattered. He said, "Certainly, friend Anansi." And he lay down beside the bamboo pole.

Anansi walked around the pole and looked at Onini from every side. He said to him, "I still can't tell which of you is longer. I have an idea. Let me tie you to the pole and stretch you as long as I can. Then we'll be able to see which one of you is longer."

Onini said, "Certainly, friend Anansi."

When Onini stretched out, Anansi spun a very thick cord and tied Onini to the bamboo pole. Then he took him up to Nyami the sky god.

When Nyami saw Onini he said, "My hands have touched him; but there remains what still remains."

So, Anansi went back down to earth. The first thing he did was to dig a huge pit in the middle of the road and cover it with leaves and grass. Then he went and hid. Before too long, Osebo started coming down the road. He wasn't really looking where he was going, and he fell into the hole. Anansi walked over and looked down. There was Osebo at the bottom of the pit. He was very upset.

"Friend Anansi, do you know who dug a pit right in the middle of the road?"

"Oh no, Uncle Osebo, I have no idea. I'm very sorry you've gotten trapped down there."

"Well, what are you going to do about it," said Osebo?

Anansi said, "Well, maybe I could help you."

Right beside the pit there was a long, springy tree. Anansi said to Osebo, "I'm going to lower this springy tree into the hole. You stick your tail up as high as you can, and I'll tie your tail to the end of the tree. Then I'll let you up very, very slowly."

Osebo said, "Thank you friend Anansi. I will not soon forget this."

When Anansi lowered the springy tree into the hole, Osebo stuck his tail up as far as he could. Anansi tied Osebo's tail to the end of the springy tree. But he didn't let him up slowly. He let go of that tree all at once, and "zing!"— Osebo flew right up to the sky god.

When Nyami saw Osebo he said, "My hands have touched him. Very well, you have won my stories, Anansi. I will get them all for you."

But as Nyami began putting all the stories into a woven bag, he thought to himself. "For too long the stories have not been in the world. I will play a trick on Anansi."

Nyami made sure that the bag he was putting the stories in was just a little bit too small. He tied it up and gave it to Anansi, who put it on his back and began climbing down toward the tree where he lived.

As he climbed down the branches of the tree, a thorn poked the bag he was carrying, and stories spilled out into the world. They went into the air. They went into the water and into the trees. They went into all of us. And now one of them is coming out of me.

Project Editor: Alice Flanagan
Design and Electronic Page Composition: Biner Design
Engraver: Liberty Photoengravers

Storytelling activities

Storytelling provides a wonderful opportunity to share information, feelings, and a love of books with children. Through listening, discussion, and a wide variety of post-story activities, children can be helped to understand new ideas, learn and use new words, practice listening skills, experience life outside the dominant culture, and develop writing and storytelling skills. Some of the following activities may be helpful in making this possible:

- Discuss the story. This will give children the opportunity to ask questions and share information they have learned.

- Ask children to retell the story. This will help you measure their comprehension and interact with them through quiet conversation.

- Ask children to act out the story. Provide generic props (scarves, crowns, masks) and puppets.

- Have paper and magic markers or crayons available so children can draw the story. You might ask them to draw a picture of one of the characters in the book or make a story map (a series of drawings reflecting the sequence of story events).

- Ask children to make cutouts of the story characters and back them with felt or flannel for use on a felt/flannel board. As you retell the story, place the cutouts on the board; then ask the children to retell the story several times. Afterwards, comment on their personal variations.

- Help children write a letter to a favorite story character; or have them pretend to be one of the characters in the story and write a letter to you.

- Ask children to tell the story from different points of view. Have them retell the story several times — each time basing it on the viewpoint of a different character.

- Play the "what if" game. Ask children to tell how the story would be different if the hero was a girl instead of a boy; if the ending changed; if the story took place today instead of "once upon a time"; if the story took place in a different country.

More about storytelling and folktales

If you'd like to read more about storytelling or other African folktales, check out some of the following books from your local library:

Breneman, Lucille N. and Bren. *Once Upon a Time: A Storytelling Handbook.* Chicago: Nelson-Hall, 1983.

Schimmel, Nancy. *Just Enough to Make a Story.* Berkeley, CA: Sisters' Choice Press, 1982.

Sierra, Judy. *Twice Upon a Time: Stories to Tell, Retell, Act Out and Write About.* New York: H. W. Wilson, 1989.

Sierra, Judy. *The Flannel Board Storytelling Book.* New York: H. W. Wilson, 1987.

Appiah, Peggy. *Anansi the Spider.* New York: Pantheon, 1966.

Arkhurst, Joyce. *The Adventures of Spider: West African Folktales.* Boston: Little Brown, 1964.

McDermott, Gerald. *Anansi the Spider Man: A Tale from the Ashanti.* New York: Holt, 1972.

Sherlock, Phillip. *Anansi the Spider Man.* New York: Harper, 1954.

Stevens, Janet. *Anansi and the Moss Covered Rock.* New York: Holiday House, 1990.

Library of Congress Cataloging-in- Publication Data
Skivington, Janice.
How Anansi obtained the sky god's stories / illustrated by Janice Skivington.
p. cm.— (Adventures in Storytelling)
Summary: In this trickster tale from West Africa, Anansi the spider sets out to retrieve all the stories of the world from Nyami, the sky god.
ISBN 0-516-05134-2
1. Anansi (Legendary character) [1. Anansi (Legendary character) 2. Folklore — Africa, West.] I. Title. II. Series.
PZB.1.S623Ho 1991
398.2 —dc20   91-7581
[E]   CIP
                                                                                              AC

Copyright © 1991 by Childrens Press ®, Inc.